FINDING PEACE: MINDFULNESS JOURNAL FOR KIDS

FINDING PEACE

MINDFULNESS
JOURNAL *for Kids*

Guided Prompts to
Help Manage Big Feelings

J. ROBIN ALBERTSON-WREN

Illustrations by Fernando Martin

ROCKRIDGE
PRESS

THIS JOURNAL
BELONGS TO:

_____

DEDICATED TO KAYLI,
who has inspired journal writing
and collecting since age two.

"Let there be peace on earth, and let it begin with me."

JILL JACKSON AND SY MILLER

CONTENTS

Introduction

WELCOME, DEAR ONE!

Every human feels many different emotions each day. Sometimes we feel frustrated or overwhelmed. We may feel sad, angry, lonely, light, or happy. We are complicated and unique human beings. No matter who you are or what is happening in your life, there are tools that you can use to feel moments of peace. This journal will teach you these amazing tools!

"Mindfulness" is paying attention to whatever is going on inside of you without judging it. When you take away the part of your thinking that says something is "good" or "bad," you can feel more relaxed about it. You can feel calm and peaceful in the middle of your busy life.

In this mindfulness journal, you can practice ways to deal with big feelings. You will learn to notice what is going on inside of you and with your emotions. You will also practice ways to feel better, stronger, calmer, kinder, and more confident.

Each section has spaces for writing or drawing your thoughts and feelings. The exercises give you tools to breathe, focus, cool down, and be yourself. You will notice that some parts of the journal are repeated. It's fun to track what changes or stays the same each time you check in.

Here we go, you amazing human.

Pause . . . Breathe . . . Peace!

GROUNDED

When we are having big feelings in our daily lives, we may feel that our minds and bodies are out of control. In these moments we need something to help us feel connected and grounded.

Imagine a tall tree. A tree can be affected by the weather around it. Rain may fall on it and wind may blow its branches. But when its roots are deep and strong, it stays upright, anchored to the ground, and does not fall. Mindfulness can help us feel strong and connected like a tree, so we can bend, but we won't break.

Anchoring Awareness

Circle the face that shows how you feel: happy, sad, surprised, worried, mad, afraid, or design your own!
Right now I feel:

Right now I can touch _____

_____ with the bottoms of my feet.

Try this meditation whenever you are feeling worried.

1. Rest your hands on top of each other on your chest.

2. Take a deep breath in and a longer breath out.

3. Notice the rise and fall of your chest and lungs.

4. Breathe in and out two more times. Keep focusing on your breathing.

What happens to your thoughts when you focus on your breathing?

_____

_____

Today, when I _____

_____**, I feel peaceful.**

Balancing

Right now I feel:

Right now I can see _____

_____ .

Sit or stand tall like a tree. Breathe in and out slowly. Close your eyes. Keep breathing. What do you notice about your balance? Focus on the top of your head and then the soles of your feet. What changes?

_____

_____

_____

_____

_____

_____

Today, _____

_____ **helps me feel balanced.**

Branching Out

Right now I feel:

Right now I can touch _____

_____.

Sit down. Breathe in and look up, and reach your hands to the sky like tall branches. Breathe out and lower your hands so that they stretch out wide to the sides. Try this three more times. How do you feel right now compared to 10 minutes ago?

_____

_____.

Tree of Love

Right now I feel:

Right now I can smell _____

_____.

This tree represents you! Fill the branches with anything you love in your life. You can add books, friends, family, games, even your favorite food. Go for it!

Planted

Right now I feel:

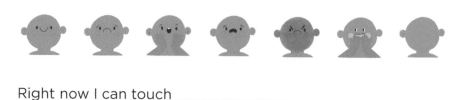

Right now I can touch _____
_____ with the bottoms of my feet.

Plant your feet on the ground.

Move your body in whatever way feels good to you, but keep your feet still.

Count to 10 and then freeze.

Think of a name for your position right now. Write it here:

_____

Today, when I move, I feel_____

_____.

New View

Right now I feel:

Right now I can hear _____

_____.

Stand in a different spot than you normally would in your room. Look around. You are getting a new view! What do you see? Does anything surprise you? Write down five things that you notice:

_____

_____

_____

_____

_____

Today, _____

_____ **helps me feel calm.**

Swirl of Feelings

Right now I feel:

Right now I can touch _____

_____.

Close your eyes. What colors do you think of when you hear the word "happy"? What about "comfortable"? Or "loved"? Draw a swirl of those colors here:

Still and Awake, Alive and Relaxed

Right now I feel:

Right now I can smell _____

_____.

**Here's a great exercise for when you are feeling over-
whelmed. You can practice it standing or sitting.
You decide!**

1. Breathe in and feel your feet on the ground. Breathe out
   and wiggle your toes.

2. Breathe in and feel where your hands are resting.
   Breathe out and close your eyes.

3. Breathe in and notice your shoulders. Breathe out and
   relax them.

4. Breathe in and open your mouth. Breathe out and smile.

How did the parts of your body change when you
breathed out?

_____

_____

_____

_____

_____

Helpful Hands

Right now I feel:

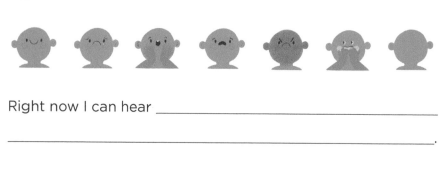

Right now I can hear _____

_____.

Wiggle your fingers. Make fists and squeeze them tight. Now shake them out. Write down five things that you like to do with your hands.

_____

_____

_____

_____

_____

Today, I feel peaceful when I _____

_____.

Fast, Slow ... Freeze!

Right now I feel:

Right now I can see _____

_____.

Find an open space (maybe outside) and move as fast as you can for 10 seconds. Then move as slowly as you can for 10 more. Then freeze. Count to 10 again.

What changes did you feel in your body when you changed speed?

_____

_____

Today, _____

_____ **helps me feel powerful.**

Mindful Eyes

Right now I feel:

Right now I can smell _____

_____ .

Focus on your sense of sight. Look out a window.

What is moving? _____

_____

What colors do you see? _____

_____

What shapes do you notice? _____

_____

What do you recognize? _____

_____

What is new? _____

_____

Today, _____

_____ **helps me feel comfortable.**

Body Check

Right now I feel:

Right now I can touch _____

_____ with the bottoms of my feet.

How do you feel in different parts of your body today?
Add drawings to show what you notice. (For example, if your
hand feels warm, you could draw a little sun there.)

Closer Look

Right now I feel:

Right now I can hear _____

_____.

Spread your fingers wide. Look closely at the tops of your hands. What do you see that you haven't noticed before?

_____

_____

Today, thinking of _____

_____ **helps me feel calm.**

Peaceful Pause

Right now I feel:

Right now I can see _____

_____.

Take a peaceful pause: Sit down. Close your eyes. Rest your hands comfortably in your lap. Keep your back straight like a tree, but not stiff. Hear your breath moving in and out. Tune in to other sounds. What do you notice?

_____

_____

_____

_____

Today, when I _____

_____**, I feel grounded.**

Noticing When

Right now I feel:

Right now I can touch _____
_____ with the bottoms of my feet.

Think for a moment: What makes you feel safe? Loved?
Strong? Happy? Write your answers here:

I feel safe when _____
_____.

I feel loved when _____
_____.

I feel strong when _____
_____.

I feel happy when _____
_____.

Today, when I _____
_____**, I feel safe.**

Happy Place

Right now I feel:

Right now I can smell _____

_____.

Draw yourself in your favorite happy place. It can be a real place or in your imagination.

What makes this your happy place?

Meadow Moment

Right now I feel:

Right now I can see _____

_____.

Imagine you are in a great big meadow. You love it here! Stand in the grass and look all around yourself.

What do you see above you? _____

What do you see below you? _____

What do you notice around you? _____

Counting Breaths

Right now I feel:

Right now I can touch _____
_____.

Bring your hands close to your face. Feel the cool air coming into your nose. Feel the warm air flowing out of your mouth. Count how long you can stay fully focused on, or "anchored," to your breathing. Write the number of breaths here:

_____

_____

Today, I feel "anchored" when I am _____
_____.

Positive Position

Right now I feel:

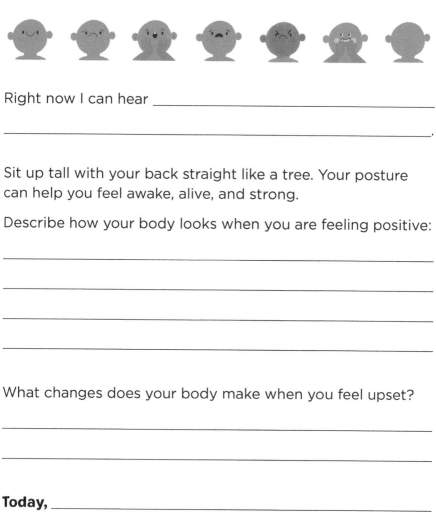

Right now I can hear _____

_____.

Sit up tall with your back straight like a tree. Your posture can help you feel awake, alive, and strong.

Describe how your body looks when you are feeling positive:

_____

_____

_____

_____

What changes does your body make when you feel upset?

_____

_____

Today, _____

_____**helps me feel relaxed.**

Strong and Connected

Right now I feel:

Right now I can see _____

_____ .

Feeling "grounded" means feeling sturdy, strong, and connected. Use the space below to draw what you picture when you think of feeling grounded:

CALM, COOL, COLLECTED

Have you ever noticed that sometimes when you get upset, you feel like you are burning up? Even though cucumbers can grow outside in the hot sun, they are one of the coolest, most refreshing vegetables. Imagine that you could stay cool and not get overheated when you are feeling big emotions. Experiment with the activities in this section to see if you can be calm and "cool as a cucumber" as you go about your daily life.

Take Five

Right now I feel:

Right now I can smell _____

_____.

Try this meditation if you are feeling frustrated or over-heated and want to calm down.

1. Close your eyes.

2. Notice five things that you can feel on your body, like warmth, texture, or pressure.

3. Next, listen for five things that you can hear.

4. Slowly blink open your eyes.

5. Now notice five things you can see.

Write three words to describe how you feel after this meditation:

_____

_____

_____

Today, _____

_____ **helps me notice what's around me.**

Chilling Out

Right now I feel:

Right now I can touch _____

_____.

Fill the space below with things that remind you of being cool. Maybe it could be something cold, like ice cubes, or "cool," like sunglasses. You decide.

Belly Breaths

Right now I feel:

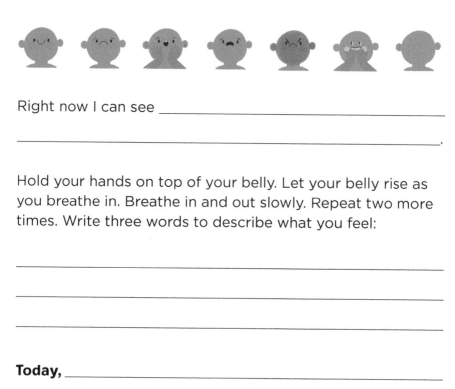

Right now I can see _____

_____.

Hold your hands on top of your belly. Let your belly rise as you breathe in. Breathe in and out slowly. Repeat two more times. Write three words to describe what you feel:

_____

_____

_____

Today, _____

_____ **helps me feel calm.**

Focused Feeling

Right now I feel:

Right now I can hear _____

_____.

Sit as still as you can. First, pay attention to your face. Next, focus on your feet. Last, focus on your hands. What do you notice?

My face feels: _____

_____

_____

My feet feel: _____

_____

_____

My hands feel: _____

_____

_____

Today, I feel happy when I _____

_____.

Under Cover

Right now I feel:

Right now I can touch _____

_____ with the bottoms of my feet.

Sit somewhere comfortable, covering yourself gently with a blanket or piece of clothing. Imagine you are sheltered like a cucumber under a leaf. Stay there for two minutes, breathing quietly.

What thoughts or images came into your mind while you were "hidden"?

_____

_____

A Plan for Calm

Right now I feel:

Right now I can hear _____

_____.

If you were helping a friend calm down, what would be your top five suggestions? Write them here:

_____

_____

_____

_____

_____

Today, when I think of _____

_____**, I feel peaceful.**

Growing Happiness

Right now I feel:

Right now I can see _____

_____.

Write your name in the cucumber. In the leaves, write words and draw pictures of things that make you happy. Color your page.

Listing Growth

Right now I feel:

Right now I can touch _____
_____.

Make a list of 10 things that grow:

_____   _____

_____   _____

_____   _____

_____   _____

_____   _____

Did you add yourself? Did you mention your feelings? You can, you know. Just like something in a garden, you grow and change every day!

Today I feel stronger when I _____
_____.

Uncurling

Right now I feel:

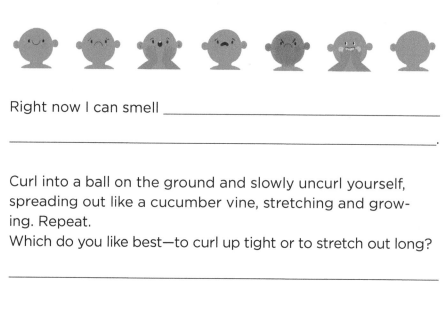

Right now I can smell _____

_____.

Curl into a ball on the ground and slowly uncurl yourself, spreading out like a cucumber vine, stretching and growing. Repeat.

Which do you like best—to curl up tight or to stretch out long?

_____

_____

Why? _____

_____

Today, I feel comfortable when I _____

_____.

Finding Your Cool

Right now I feel:

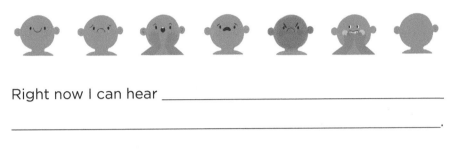

Right now I can hear _____

_____.

Think of a time when you almost lost your cool. What helped you feel in control again? Write your answer here:

_____

_____

Today, when I _____

_____**, I can cool down.**

Alive!

Right now I feel:

Right now I can see _____

_____ .

Cucumbers need sun and rain to grow. Draw a picture of yourself surrounded by all the things you need to stay alive and grow. You might want to add things like water, food, sleep, or exercise.

Mindful Eating

Right now I feel:

Right now I can smell _____

_____.

Try this meditation when your thoughts are racing and you want to slow down your body and mind.

1. Choose a piece of food. (Ask a grown-up for a piece of fruit or a cracker . . . or a cucumber!)

2. Sit quietly and look closely at your item. Describe it.

3. Does it have a smell?

4. If you rub it between your fingers, does it make a sound?

5. Take one bite and hold it in your mouth.

6. Chew, taste, and swallow very slowly.

Write three words that describe your food: _____

_____

_____

Today, _____

_____ **helps me feel relaxed.**

Super Slow

Right now I feel:

Right now I can touch _____

_____.

You can move and cool down at the same time. Practice lifting your arm super slowly in the air. Raise it to your shoulder. Wait a minute, then lower it super slowly.

Write down four things you noticed as you moved:

_____

_____

_____

_____

Today, I feel calm when I _____

_____.

Spreading Care and Peace

Right now I feel:

Right now I can hear _____

_____.

One cucumber seed can grow to make a lot of cucumbers to feed many people. Make a list of things you can do to care for and bring a sense of peace to other people:

_____

_____

_____

_____

_____

Today, _____

_____ **helps me feel happy.**

Stepping Up

Right now I feel:

Right now I can touch _____

_____ with the bottoms of my feet.

Breathe in as you lift one foot. Breathe out as you lower your foot. Do this again slowly 10 times.

Describe this activity. Was it hard or easy to breathe while you were moving? Could you find a rhythm?

_____

_____

Today, _____

_____ **makes me smile.**

Safe and Sound

Right now I feel:

Right now I can smell _____
_____.

Think about all the things that make you feel safe and comfortable in your life.

Write or draw pictures of those things here:

Tough Skin

Right now I feel:

Right now I can touch _____

_____.

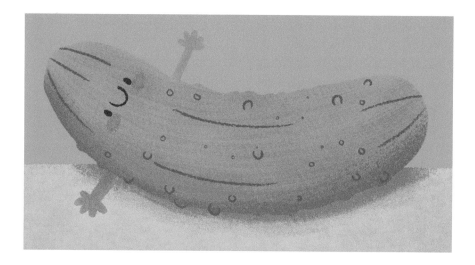

Cucumbers can grow a thick, bumpy skin to protect them-selves from insects and stormy weather. What do you do to protect yourself from staying upset by things that "bug" you?

Write a list here:

_____

_____

_____

Pickles!

Right now I feel:

Right now I can see _____

_____.

Did you know that when you add vinegar and other spices to cucumbers, they become pickles?

Pickles can have different flavors. If you were a pickle, would you want to be sweet or sour?

_____

Why?

_____

_____

Today, when I _____

_____**, I have energy!**

Space to Move

Right now I feel:

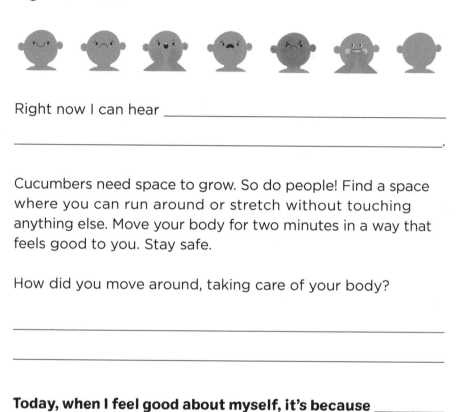

Right now I can hear _____
_____.

Cucumbers need space to grow. So do people! Find a space where you can run around or stretch without touching anything else. Move your body for two minutes in a way that feels good to you. Stay safe.

How did you move around, taking care of your body?

_____

_____

Today, when I feel good about myself, it's because _____
_____.

Labeling Love

Right now I feel:

Right now I can see _____

_____.

Fill the pickle jars with groups of things you love. Label the jars. (They could be called "games," "people," "foods," or something else. You decide!)

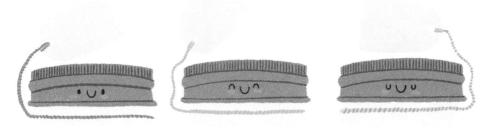

FOCUSED

In many parts of the world, when the air is humid at night, you can see fireflies flickering in the darkness. They are like tiny flashlights blinking off and on. Focusing on their twinkling lights can feel very peaceful. There are many other things you can focus on to help you manage big feelings. Let's "shine the light" on some of those activities!

Tuning In

Right now I feel:

Right now I can smell _____

_____.

Look closely at one of your hands. Focus on the inside of that hand. See the lines there? Trace them with your finger and count them.

How many lines did you count?

_____

Today, I feel peaceful when I _____

_____.

Listening Ears

Right now I feel:

Right now I can see _____

_____.

Try this meditation if you are feeling distracted, confused, or upset. Focusing on sounds can help you feel grounded and more relaxed.

1. Close your eyes and listen.

2. Focus on the sounds around you and let your thoughts relax.

3. Notice sounds that are far away.

4. Notice sounds that are close to you.

5. Can you hear the sound of your own quiet breathing?

List five sounds that you hear:

_____

_____

_____

Today, _____

_____ **helps me focus.**

Where's the Spotlight?

Right now I feel:

Right now I can touch _____

_____.

In the dark, fireflies' light draws your attention. What is on your mind today? What is trying to get your attention?

_____

_____

Breathe in and out three times slowly. Push your attention away from your thoughts and focus on your body. Just notice yourself breathing in and out.

Today, when _____

_____**, I feel relaxed.**

Flickering Attention

Right now I feel:

Right now I can hear _____

_____.

Flicker your attention off and on like a firefly. Look around. Name five things out loud that you can see. Close your eyes and count slowly to five. Open your eyes and notice five new things. Repeat.

Name something interesting that you noticed:

_____

Today, _____

_____ **made me smile.**

Mindful Mosaic

Right now I feel:

Right now I can smell _____

_____ .

This kind of picture is called a mosaic. Take as much time as you want to carefully color it in.

Light It Up

Right now I feel:

Right now I can touch _____

_____ with the bottoms of my feet.

Fireflies show their light so other fireflies will notice them and want to be near them. What do you do that makes other people want to be around you?

_____

_____

Today, something I like about myself is _____

_____.

Amazing You!

Right now I feel:

Right now I can see _____
_____.

Close your eyes and picture yourself doing something you love to do. Smile! You are amazing! Make a list of all the things you are good at:

_____

_____

_____

_____

_____

Today, I feel peaceful when I _____
_____.

Words of Support

Right now I feel:

Right now I can hear _____

_____.

People use words to be kind to others and to support one another. What are some words you like to hear that make you feel loved?

_____

_____

Today, I like that I can _____

_____.

Shine On!

Right now I feel:

Right now I can touch _____

_____.

Draw a picture of yourself with light shining out around you, like a firefly. Imagine your light is the color of peace. What color(s) will you use?

Leading Light

Right now I feel:

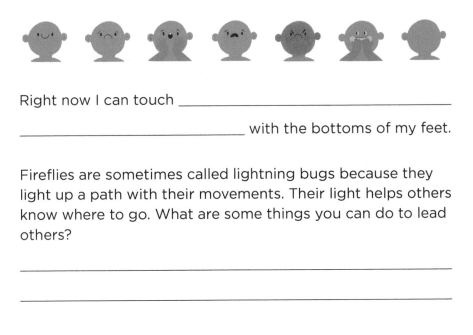

Right now I can touch _____

_____ with the bottoms of my feet.

Fireflies are sometimes called lightning bugs because they light up a path with their movements. Their light helps others know where to go. What are some things you can do to lead others?

_____

_____

Today, when I _____

_____**, I feel peaceful.**

Star Breathing

Right now I feel:

Right now I can see _____

_____.

Use this meditation to help you feel focused and peaceful, any day, any time.

1. Spread your fingers wide. Imagine your hand is a firefly glowing like a star.

2. Trace the outside of your fingers using your other hand, like this:

   • Breathe in and move your finger up the outside of your "star" hand.

   • When you get to the top of your finger, hold your breath for a second.

   • Then move down the other side of your finger, breathing out.

   • Continue, following the outline of your whole hand.

Today, this breathing exercise made me feel _____

_____.

Off and On

Right now I feel:

Right now I can touch _____

_____.

A firefly's light comes and goes, just like our feelings. Think of a time when you were sad. What happened to make you feel better?

_____

_____

Think of a time when you felt happy. What made you feel that way?

_____

_____

Today, I have lots of energy when I _____

_____.

Again and Again

Right now I feel:

Right now I can hear _____

_____ .

 A pattern is anything that repeats over and over. Patterns of light, sound, color, and movement are all around us. Are there any patterns you notice around you?

_____

_____

 Is there anything in your life that repeats over and over? Is it something you wish you could change?

_____

_____

Color for Peace

Right now I feel:

Right now I can touch _____

_____ with the bottoms of my feet.

This kind of circle is called a mandala. The design starts in the center and moves toward the outside. Coloring in all these little patterns can help you settle your thoughts and emotions.

Bright and Alert

Right now I feel:

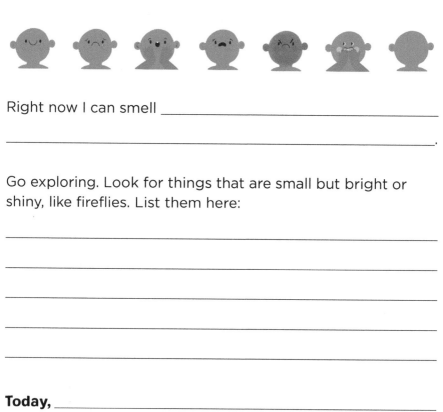

Right now I can smell _____

_____.

Go exploring. Look for things that are small but bright or shiny, like fireflies. List them here:

_____

_____

_____

_____

_____

Today, _____

_____ **makes me feel like I glow on the inside.**

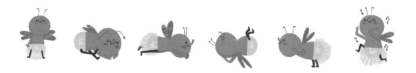

Shh . . .

Right now I feel:

Right now I can see _____

_____.

Fireflies are silent in the night sky. Try to move around for three minutes without making a sound.

What made this activity hard?

_____

What did you like about moving silently?

_____

Today, I am glad that _____

_____ **helps me feel peaceful.**

Zooming In

Right now I feel:

Right now I can touch _____

_____.

Find something interesting that you would like to draw.
It should be something with small details. What is it?

_____

Now zoom in with your eyes, like you are looking through a
magnifying glass, and draw part of it, really big, right here:

Gentle Approach

Right now I feel:

Right now I can hear _____

_____.

Fireflies are very light. You can barely feel them when they land on you. See how close you can get your hand to your face without touching it. Can you feel warmth? Is it itchy? Close your eyes and try it again. What do you notice?

_____

_____

Today, I feel happiness inside when I _____

_____.

Taking Temperature

Right now I feel:

Right now I can touch _____

_____ with the bottoms of my feet.

Think about things that are hot and cold. Go on a hunt
for things that make you feel warm (like the light of a fire).
Make a list of them here:

_____

_____

_____

Today, when I am still, I feel_____

_____.

Artistic Awareness

Right now I feel:

Right now I can see _____

_____.

Create your own drawing page. Make a dot on your page, and then, without lifting your pencil up, make squiggly lines all around the space below. Then color in the shapes you made.

KIND

Capybaras are peaceful and kind mammals that live in South America. They are very mindful creatures who pay attention to their surroundings and stay alert. Capybaras are comfortable being alone but also love to gather in herds. Enjoy these mindfulness exercises to help you experience loving kindness and awareness, like a gentle capybara.

Wonderful You!

Right now I feel:

Right now I can touch _____

_____ with the bottoms of my feet.

Try this meditation whenever you are feeling sad or lonely.

1. Stand in front of a mirror and make a silly face.

2. Smile.

3. Raise your hands above your head.

4. Say: "Hello, wonderful you!"

When we open our body up and send ourselves kind wishes, we tell our body and mind that we are safe and happy.

How did your feelings change when you stopped to grin at yourself in the mirror?

_____

_____

You can even enjoy this exercise on a day when you are already feeling happy!

Today, when _____

_____**, I feel loved.**

Heads Up

Right now I feel:

Right now I can see _____

_____.

When capybaras swim, their faces stay above water so they can see plants and other creatures. Go exploring and notice things that are green. Write them down here:

_____

_____

_____

_____

_____

_____

Today, _____

_____ **helps me feel happy.**

Mindful Movement

Right now I feel:

Right now I can touch _____

_____.

Try lifting your right arm up at the same time that you lift your right leg. Now try moving your left arm and your left leg at the same time. Move across the room this way.

Now move your right arm at the same time as your left leg, and your left arm with your right leg.

Which felt more comfortable? How do you think a capybara moves?

_____

_____.

Go Team!

Right now I feel:

Right now I can hear _____
_____ .

Capybaras move in herds, like a team.

When people work as a team, they can:

_____
_____ .

Who Is in Your Herd?

Right now I feel:

Right now I can smell _____

_____.

Capybaras like to be around other capybaras in the herd. Draw a picture of your "herd" here. Who do you most want to be around?

Sense of Smell

Right now I feel:

Right now I can touch _____

_____ with the bottoms of my feet.

There are many ways to find happiness. What are some smells that make you feel happy?

_____

_____

_____

_____

_____

_____

Today, _____

_____ **helps me find peace.**

Listing Love

Right now I feel:

Right now I can see _____

_____.

Think of somebody you love to be around. What are five
things that you love about them? List those things here:

_____

_____

_____

_____

_____

Today, I notice kindness when _____

_____.

Remembering Kindness

Right now I feel:

Right now I can hear _____

_____.

Think about a time that someone did something kind
for you.

What was it?

_____

_____

How did it make you feel then?

_____

_____

When you think about it now, how does it make you feel?

_____

_____

Today, I am thankful for _____

_____.

Best Foot Forward

Right now I feel:

Right now I can touch _____

_____.

Fill the foot outline with drawings or words to show what you can feel with your feet.

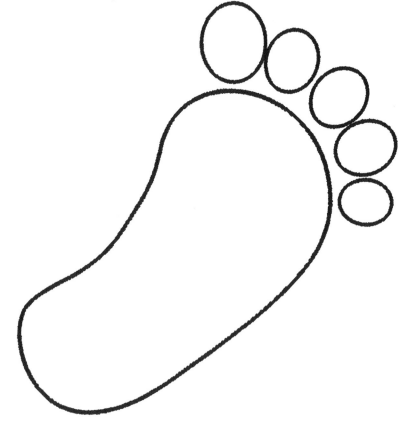

Loving Kindness

Right now I feel:

Right now I can smell _____

_____.

Try this meditation when you are feeling annoyed or worried.

1. Think of someone who is easy for you to be around.

2. Close your eyes and imagine them doing something they love to do.

3. Where are they? Who is with them? Are they smiling or laughing?

4. Speak these sentences out loud as you picture them in your head: "May you be happy. May you be healthy. May you stay safe. May you feel peaceful."

Who did you think of? _____

Today, this activity made me feel _____

_____.

On Your Own

Right now I feel:

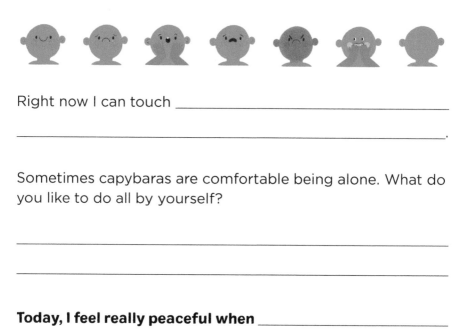

Right now I can touch _____

_____ .

Sometimes capybaras are comfortable being alone. What do you like to do all by yourself?

_____

_____

Today, I feel really peaceful when _____

_____ .

Dear Me

Right now I feel:

Right now I can see _____

_____.

You are the person you know best in the whole world. What do you like about yourself? Make your list here:

Dear Me,

Here are some of the things I like about you:

- You are _____.

- You can _____.

- You are _____.

- You can _____.

- You are _____.

Today, _____

_____ **helps me feel peaceful and loved.**

Patience

Right now I feel:

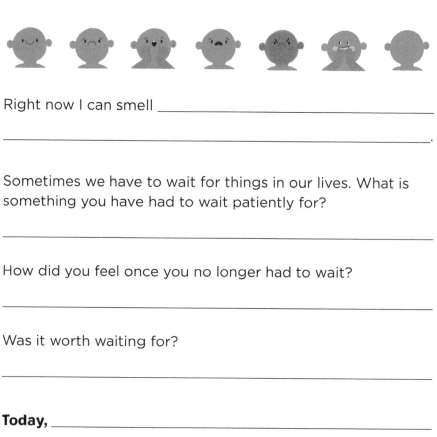

Right now I can smell _____

_____.

Sometimes we have to wait for things in our lives. What is something you have had to wait patiently for?

_____

How did you feel once you no longer had to wait?

_____

Was it worth waiting for?

_____

Today, _____

_____ **helps me be patient.**

Love It!

Right now I feel:

Right now I can touch _____
_____ with the bottoms of my feet.

Fill the heart with whatever colors you choose. Add your own hearts around the edges.

Low Down

Right now I feel:

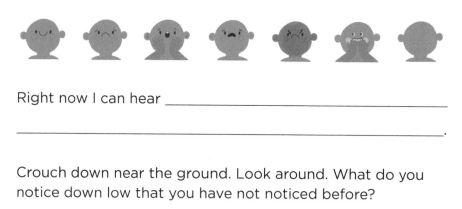

Right now I can hear _____
_____.

Crouch down near the ground. Look around. What do you notice down low that you have not noticed before?

_____

_____

Did you find anything that you thought was lost?

_____

_____

Today, _____
_____ **helps me notice the world around me.**

Mindful Listening

Right now I feel:

Right now I can see _____

_____.

Listen closely with your mindful ears like an alert capybara. What sounds do you hear?

Write your answers here:

Loud sound: _____

Quiet sound: _____

Far away sound: _____

Close sound: _____

Nature sound: _____

Machine sound: _____

Person sound: _____

Today, _____

_____ **helps my mind feel peaceful.**

Colors of Life

Right now I feel:

Right now I can smell _____

_____.

If friendship was a color, what would it be?

_____

If love was a color, what would it be?

_____

Draw a page filled with love and friendship, however it looks to you:

Kind Thoughts

Right now I feel:

Right now I can see _____

_____.

Imagine this capybara is thinking kind thoughts. What is it wishing it could say to you to make you feel loved and cared for? Fill in the thought bubble.

Noting Kindness

Right now I feel:

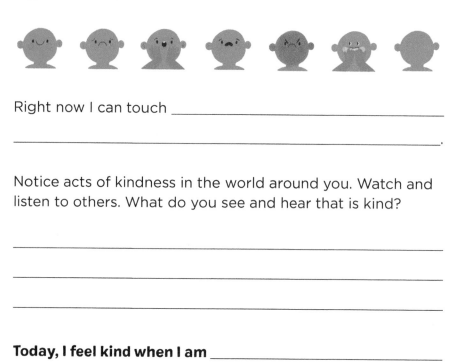

Right now I can touch _____

_____.

Notice acts of kindness in the world around you. Watch and listen to others. What do you see and hear that is kind?

_____

_____

_____

Today, I feel kind when I am _____

_____.

Happy Hearts

Right now I feel:

Right now I can hear _____

_____.

Fill the page with hearts and smiley faces. Next to each one, write the name of a person you like, a thing you like, or something you like to do.

CONNECTED

Did you know that the air on Earth is the same air that dinosaurs breathed millions of years ago? Amazing! We are all connected through the air we breathe. Focusing on our breathing can help us feel connected to the world and to all living things around us.

Love Life

Right now I feel:

Right now I can see _____

_____ .

Try this meditation when you want to calm down or cheer up.

1. Sit down. Get comfortable. Take a deep breath in through your nose.

2. Breathe out more slowly through your mouth.

3. Breathe in through your nose again. When you do, think the word "LOVE."

4. Breathe out and think "LIFE."

5. Keep going. Your only job is to breathe in "LOVE" and breathe out "LIFE."

How did it feel to match your breaths with words?

_____

A Grateful Heart

Right now I feel:

Right now I can touch _____

_____ .

This is a gratitude heart. Fill it with words and drawings that show all the things you are glad for in your life.

Breathing Out

Right now I feel:

Right now I can smell _____

_____.

Hold up one finger. Imagine that it is a candle. Take a deep breath in and blow out the candle. Try it again, using longer and longer breaths out.

What changed when your out-breath was longer than your in-breath?

_____

_____

Today, _____

_____ **helps me feel peaceful.**

Rainbow Arms

Right now I feel:

Right now I can hear _____

_____.

Press your hands together near your heart. Breathe in, look up, and lift your hands to the sky. Breathe out, and stretch your hands wide, moving them out and down like a rainbow. How does it feel to breathe with rainbow arms?

_____

Today, thinking of _____

_____ **made me feel relaxed.**

Special Someone

Right now I feel:

Right now I can touch _____

_____ with the bottoms of my feet.

Think of someone in your life who has done something nice for you. Think of the time they spent on YOU, making your life better. Write their name here:

_____

Go thank them, or write a note and send it to them.

Blown Away

Right now I feel:

Right now I can hear _____

_____.

Imagine what an angry thought would look like. Try to draw some below. Then add a swirling breath of good thoughts that blow the angry ones off the page.

Slow and Steady

Right now I feel:

Right now I can see _____

_____.

Set a timer for one minute and breathe normally. See how many breaths you take. Set it again and breathe more slowly. See how long you can make each breath last. (Keep breathing. Don't hold your breath!) Can you slow your breathing down any more?

Fill in the blanks:

Normally, I take _____ breaths in one minute.

The second time, I took _____ breaths in one minute.

The third time, I took _____ breaths in one minute.

Today, I love doing _____

_____

_____.

Float and Breathe

Right now I feel:

Right now I can touch _____
_____.

Go outside and find a leaf. Take a deep breath in and lift the leaf up high. Let the leaf go and see if you can breathe out for the same amount of time it takes it to reach the ground. Then try it again.

What happened?

_____
_____.

Happy Smells

Right now I feel:

Right now I can smell _____

_____.

Think about a time you smelled something delicious. (Maybe it's right now!) Where did it come from? Did someone make it? Take a moment to remember and to whisper out loud, "Thank you for that happy moment."

Describe your memory:

_____

_____

_____

_____

Today, I feel comfortable when I _____

_____.

Words to Breathe

Right now I feel:

Right now I can hear _____

_____.

Remember how you breathed in "LOVE" and "LIFE" earlier? Today, choose your own words. What words do you want to think as you breathe in and out?

Do this three times, and then write down your words below:

Breathe in:

_____

_____

Breathe out:

_____

_____

Today, when I _____
_____**, I can cool down.**

Make a Wish!

Right now I feel:

Right now I can touch _____

_____ with the bottoms of my feet.

Decorate the cupcake. Add candles. Make a wish as you blow them out.

What did you wish for? If you want to, you can write it down. (It's okay to keep it a secret, too!)

I wished:

_____.

Help for Humanity

Right now I feel:

Right now I can see _____

_____.

People are taking care of each other all around the world. Make a list of some things that humans do daily that help other living things:

Here are some to get you started:

1. Farmers grow food.

2. I pick up trash.

3. _____

4. _____

5. _____

6. _____

Today, _____

_____ **helps me feel connected.**

Favorite Words

Right now I feel:

Right now I can touch _____

_____.

The words we speak affect others. Find someone to help you make a list of all the kind and helpful words you can think of in two minutes. Write some of your favorite words here:

_____

_____

_____

_____

Today, I feel connected to the world around me when I _____

_____

_____.

Come and Go

Right now I feel:

Right now I can see _____

_____.

Feelings come and go, just like bubbles. Fill the bubbles with words and drawings to name all the feelings you have felt since you first opened this journal.

Nose to Knees

Right now I feel:

Right now I can hear _____

_____.

Sit on the floor with one leg laid out in front of you. Reach your arms up, breathing in. Bend forward as you breathe out. Can you touch your toes? Breathe in, stretching up. Breathe out, reaching your nose to your knee. How did this make you feel?

_____

_____

"May I . . ."

Right now I feel:

Right now I can smell _____

_____.

Imagine yourself in a place you love, with people and animals you love, doing something you love. Breathe in and out. With every deep breath in, send yourself a wish:

"May I be happy."

"May I be healthy."

"May I stay safe."

"May I feel peaceful."

Where did you imagine yourself?

_____

Who was with you?

_____

Today, _____

_____ **makes me feel loved.**

Holding On and Letting Go

Right now I feel:

Right now I can touch _____

_____.

Draw a picture of yourself holding balloons. Imagine the balloons are thoughts and feelings that you want to hold on to. Now add some clouds. Imagine these are thoughts and feelings you want to let go.

Tools for Big Emotions

Right now I feel:

Right now I can see _____

_____.

Everybody has difficult moments. Sometimes we are sad, frustrated, confused, or lonely. Other times we feel happy and light. All of these feelings are part of being human. You have tools to help you move, breathe, focus, and notice these feelings so you can find moments of peace every day.

List some of your tools. Here are two to get you started:

1. I can focus on my breath moving in and out of my body.

2. I can remember all the people who love me.

3. _____

4. _____

5. _____

Today, I know it is okay to feel big feelings, like_____

_____

_____**, because I am human, and I have tools to help me.**

Scoop Up the Love

Right now I feel:

Right now I can hear _____

_____.

Imagine the ground underneath you is covered in love. Reach down and scoop up the love in your arms. Take a deep breath in and fling the love into the air. Let it travel through the air all around you. Keep going.

What else would you like to imagine spreading through the air to people all around the world?

_____

_____

_____

_____

Today, when I feel good about myself, it's because _____

_____.

Gratitude List

Right now I feel:

Right now I can see _____.

Try this meditation before going to sleep at night:

1. Set a timer for two minutes.

2. Write down all the things you can think of that you are thankful for in your amazing life (even if things are hard sometimes).

3. Think of people, animals, activities, foods, and things in nature. Which ones make you feel peaceful and connected to the world? (You can even add this journal.)

4. When you're done, show your family your list. See if they want to try it, too.

5. Make a list for your home that everyone can add to during the month!

_____

_____

_____

Today, _____

_____ **makes me feel peaceful inside.**

Acknowledgments

I'm so grateful to Mindful Schools for their training of educators around the world and for their work with children, developing attention, resilience, and compassion in schools, as they help build awareness, transform lives, and bring positive change to communities.

About the Author

J. ROBIN ALBERTSON-WREN loves teaching children and adults—she's been doing it for over 20 years! She is the author of *Mindfulness for Kids: 30 Fun Activities to Stay Calm, Happy and in Control*. She spends her days teaching outdoor forest-preschool to young students, hiking trails, and practicing mindfulness in nature. She also teaches online courses for the Contemplative Sciences Center and the School of Education and Human Development at the University of Virginia. She loves reading and writing and keeps her own happiness journal by her pillow. Learn more at Mind-Awake.weebly.com.